THE FIRST
CHRISTMAS
in ORIGAMI

Geneva Cobb Iijima

Publishers Since 1798

THOMAS NELSON PUBLISHERS

Nashville

*I dedicate this book to my husband,
Peter, who grew up in Japan.
Because of him I was introduced to
the beautiful art of origami.*

Copyright © 1993 by Geneva Iijima.

Published in Nashville, Tennessee, by Thomas Nelson, Inc., Publishers, and distributed in Canada by Word Communications, Ltd., Richmond, British Columbia, and in the United Kingdom by Word (UK), Ltd., Milton Keynes, England.

Scripture quotations are from the NEW KING JAMES VERSION of the Bible. Copyright © 1979, 1980, 1982, Thomas Nelson, Inc., Publishers.

Library of Congress Cataloging-in-Publication Data

Iijima, Geneva Cobb.
   The first Christmas in origami / Geneva Cobb Iijima.
     p. cm.
   ISBN 0-8407-3544-8 (pb)
   1. Origami. 2. Crèches (Nativity scenes) 3. Jesus Christ—Nativity. I. Title.
TT870.I54 1993
736'.982—dc20
                                                           93-13173
                                                              CIP

Printed in the United States of America
3 4 5 6 7 - 99 98 97 96 95

Contents

Introduction 4

A Visit from an Angel 7

Mary Faces Unbelief 13

Mary Sees a Miracle 19

Joseph's Visitor 27

An Unexpected Journey 33

The Shining Moment 39

The Shepherds' Surprise 45

A Visit to the Temple 53

Wise Men and a Star 59

God Protects the Infant King 65

Stable 70

About the Author 72

Introduction

The First Christmas in Origami provides an opportunity for families to experience the joy of Christmas in a brand new way—by creatively depicting the familiar story through the ancient art of paper folding. The nativity set you create will become a part of your Christmas celebrations, delighting you and your guests throughout the season.

The ageless stories accompanying each origami figure come alive with vivid detail through the sights and sounds of ancient Palestine. Mary's fears, her rapture, and Joseph's turmoil, as well as his anger over having to make a trip at such a time, give readers a new perspective on the long-ago events of Christmas.

Japanese origami accents the simplicity of the biblical account. By working together on each origami figure (struggling at times to get the folds right) a family will bond in a creative learning experience. Adults who never thought they could do origami will find they can, if they persevere. Children who may have tried it in school will enjoy teaching their parents.

Origami has delighted families for generations. It's my prayer that through this book your family will discover both the joy of origami and the beauty of Christ's nativity this Christmas season.

How to Use This Book

The ten stories with their accompanying origami figures in this book are designed as an Advent family* activity to be used two or three evenings a week during the weeks before Christmas. Read the story as a family. Then work together on the origami figure. Make the stable in the back of the book first, and fill it with the figures as you complete them.

---

*This book can easily be adapted for classroom use. Each child can make his or her own figures, resulting in a complete nativity set to be taken home.

If origami is new to you, relax. The paper is surprisingly stretchable and refoldable. As you succeed with the simple figures, you'll build confidence that will help you with the more difficult ones. You *can* do it! If you have to throw away a piece and start over, don't fret. Take your time and try again.

Paper

You may use any kind of thin, foldable paper to make the figures in this book. Christmas wrap (usually foil or solid color), light weight brown wrapping paper, colored butcher paper, computer or typing paper, or the usual origami paper are all satisfactory. Even aluminum foil works fine for the angel or star. If you cut your own paper, it's essential that you cut straight edges and corners.

If you choose packaged origami paper, you may find it in craft, stationery, or art stores. In addition, it is often located in the art section of department stores.

Symbols and Terms

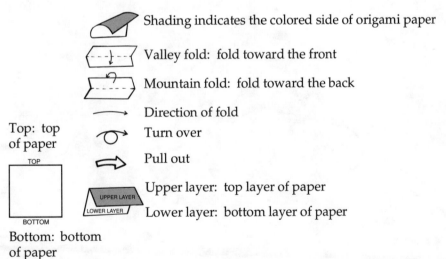

Shading indicates the colored side of origami paper

Valley fold: fold toward the front

Mountain fold: fold toward the back

Direction of fold

Top: top
of paper

Turn over

Pull out

Upper layer: top layer of paper

Lower layer: bottom layer of paper

Bottom: bottom
of paper

A Visit from an Angel

E vening shadows lengthened. Here and there along the main street, women carried their clay pitchers toward the well on the edge of the village.

Mary laid aside the coat she was sewing for her father. Then she grabbed her water jug and dashed outside as she heard her friend Ruth calling her name. Going to the well was the social event of the day, and in the Galilean foothills town of Nazareth, life was hard. There wasn't much to do for fun.

Ruth smiled, as they fell into step together. "Have you seen Joseph lately?" she asked.

Mary blushed. "He came over to talk with Father a while last night."

"Did they decide on a wedding date?"

"Oh, not yet. The betrothal dinner was only a month ago," Mary replied, laughing. "You know it usually takes a year to prepare for a marriage. I haven't even started sewing the wedding clothes yet."

"I'll help you," Ruth offered. "Oh, I can hardly wait! A wedding is so exciting—feasting for a whole week. It's about the only important event that ever happens around here. Do you suppose your relatives from Judea will come?"

Mary nodded.

"You're a lucky girl. Joseph is so strong and kind." Then she winked, "And handsome too."

Mary blushed. "I'm very blessed," she said.

"There's no better carpenter in all Galilee," Ruth assured her.

When they arrived at the well, the girls drew their water and were adjusting the jugs on their heads, when Ruth gasped and her face drained of color. The setting sun reflected off the armor of several Roman soldiers in the distance. "I hate them," she whispered. "If only the Messiah would come. He would drive out the Romans."

"They're going on," Mary reassured her. The girls turned and hurried home, their happiness gone.

Before they parted, however, Mary looked at Ruth and said earnestly, "Did you hear the rabbi say on the sabbath that the Messiah's coming is near?"

"I certainly hope so," answered Ruth. Then just before she disappeared around the corner toward her house she turned. "Sometimes I wonder if He will come at all. I mean, we've waited so long. Do you really think He will?"

"Oh, yes!" Mary assured her. "The rabbi said the time is right. I can hardly wait to see Him!"

The sun sank behind the distant hills and darkness fell across the landscape as Mary remembered the rabbi's comments. He had said the Messiah would be born of a virgin in David's family line. *That's my family. Perhaps I will be. . . . No, not way up here in Nazareth. Everything of importance happens in Jerusalem, or do the Scriptures say something about Bethlehem? Well, that's only five miles from Jerusalem.*

Suddenly, a bright light shone around her, and a glorious creature in dazzling white robes stood before her. Terrified, Mary fell at his feet.

"Rejoice, highly favored one, the Lord is with you," he announced. "You will conceive in your womb and bring forth a Son, and shall call His name JESUS. He will be great, and will be called the

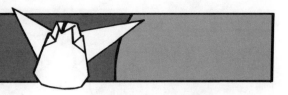

Son of the Highest; and the Lord God will give Him the throne of His father David. And . . . of His kingdom there will be no end."[*]

Mary's mind whirled. "How will this happen?" she blurted out. "I'm not even married yet!"

"The Holy Spirit will come upon you," explained the angel. "That Holy One who is to be born will be called the Son of God."[†]

Then the angel told her some more exciting news. "People thought your relative Elizabeth was too old to have a baby, but nothing is impossible with God. She is now six months pregnant."

"May it come about as you have said," Mary whispered in awe. Even as she said it, her heart sang for joy. God had a plan for *her*. He had chosen her for a unique purpose.

God has a special plan for every one of His creations.
Like Mary, however, we all need to give Him
permission to work out that plan in us.

Paper suggestions:
White paper or silver or gold foil
Size: 9 x 9 inches

---

[*]Luke 1:28, 30b–33.
[†]Luke 1:35.

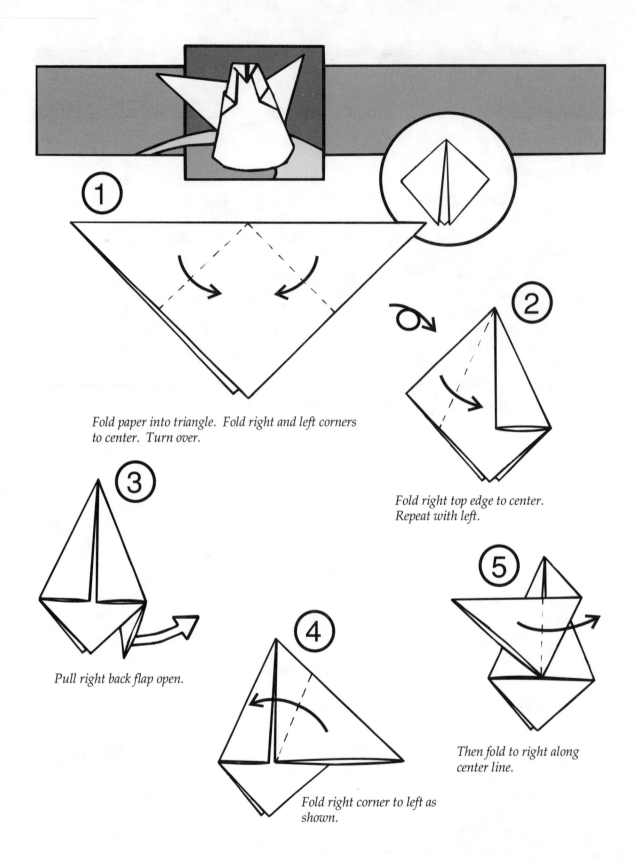

① Fold paper into triangle. Fold right and left corners to center. Turn over.

② Fold right top edge to center. Repeat with left.

③ Pull right back flap open.

④ Fold right corner to left as shown.

⑤ Then fold to right along center line.

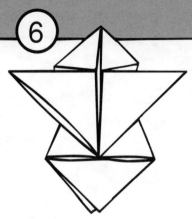

Repeat steps 3, 4, and 5 with
left corner.

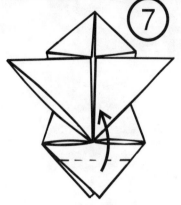

Fold upper layer of bottom corner
along fold line.

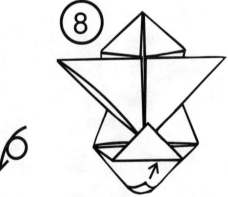

Tuck lower layer of bottom corner
inside. Turn over.

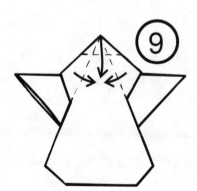

Fold top right flap forward. Repeat with left.
Fold top point down for head.

Separate front and back sides, if you
wish the angel to stand.

Mary Faces Unbelief

After the angel left, God's holy presence descended upon the room in a way Mary could not explain in all the years that followed. She simply knew that something happened that forever changed her life. Awed, she lay on her face for a long time and eventually drifted into a peaceful sleep.

The following morning Mary could think of nothing but the angel's visit. As she returned from the well, she tripped on a tree root and sloshed out most of her jar of water giving herself a good drenching. At breakfast her father called her name three times before she heard him ask for the goat cheese from the cellar, and she stabbed her finger several times when she and Mother were mending.

"Mary, whatever is on your mind?" her mother finally asked.

Mary looked at her thoughtfully. "Mother, have you ever seen an angel?"

Her mother shook her head, surprised. "Why do you ask, Mary?"

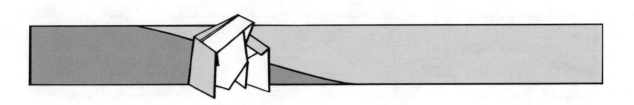

As Mary excitedly related her story of the angel visit, her mother's eyes lit up. "Is it possible that you are to be the mother of the Messiah?" she asked in wonder.

Then, as if having second thoughts Mary's mother added, "The Messiah will come someday, that's true, but I fear you've been thinking too much about it, Mary. Maybe you were only dreaming. You said you fell asleep. Yes, that must be it," she continued thoughtfully. "And I fear you've been alone too much lately. You should ask Ruth to come over soon and begin working on your wedding clothes."

Her mother's words pierced Mary like darts, and she looked away, hurt. Then her courage returned. "I know it sounds strange, Mother. I know nothing like this has happened before, but it has happened now. And the angel gave me a sign. He said Elizabeth is expecting a child too."

Her mother, still puzzled, shook her gray head. "Now, Mary, you know Elizabeth is much too old to bear a child. You were just dreaming."

At supper Mary repeated the story for her father. "When the Messiah comes, Mary, will He be born into a poor home such as mine? Surely the Messiah deserves more than I have to offer," he said, gesturing with his hands and ending the discussion.

Mary tossed on her pallet all night long. "They don't believe me. My own parents really don't believe me!" she repeated over and over. If only she could talk with someone who would understand.

Joseph! He was her betrothed. He seemed so kind and good. Surely he would understand! Of course, they had never talked at length, but she decided to try at the very first opportunity.

It was several days before the opportunity presented itself. However, when Joseph dropped by to talk with her father, Mary cornered him first and plunged into her story.

"Mary," he said, "I'm eager for the Messiah to come, too, but we can't dream Him here!"

Earnestly she reminded him of angel appearances throughout the Old Testament and of the prophecies that the Messiah would be

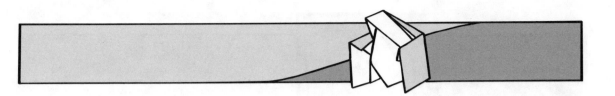

born of a virgin. He only shook his head and left, forgetting that he had come to see her father.

Stunned, Mary watched him go. *Why is it so difficult for those I love to trust my word?* she wondered. She leaned her head against the cool limestone wall and cried. "God, I need someone who will believe, someone who will understand."

Then she remembered Elizabeth!

Like Mary, you too may sometimes feel no one understands.
But God always understands,
and He will help you as He did Mary.

Paper suggestions:
Origami or wrapping paper
Size: 6 x 6 inches

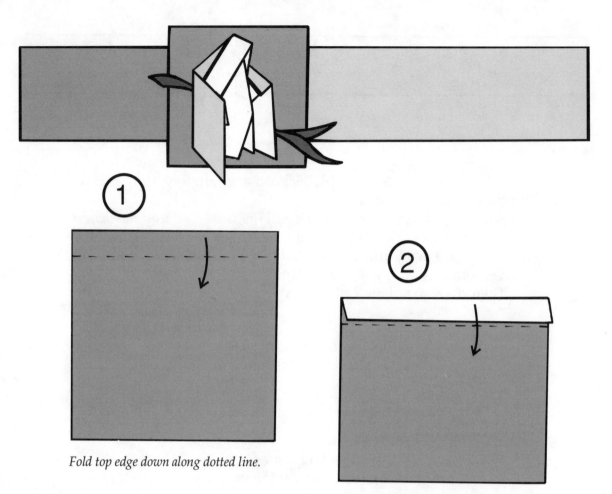

① Fold top edge down along dotted line.

② Fold down again on dotted line.

③ Fold vertically along center line and reopen. Turn over.

④ Fold right and left corners down as shown.

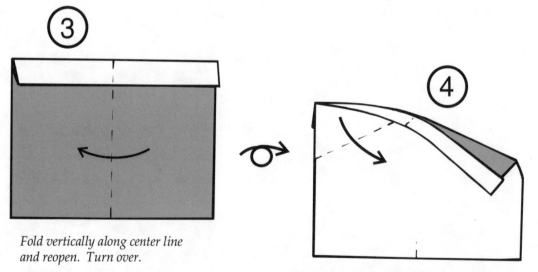

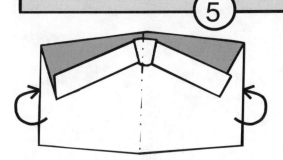

(5)

(6)

Make mountain fold along broken line.

Fold upper layer down along dotted line. Turn over and repeat.

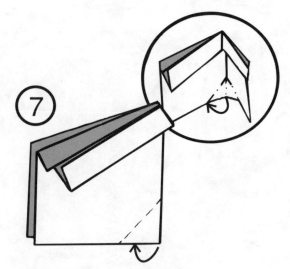

(7)

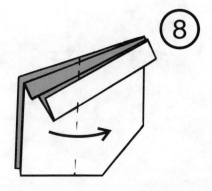

(8)

Fold right bottom corner inside.

Fold upper left layer to right edge. Turn over and repeat.

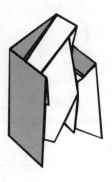

Mary Sees
a Miracle

A week later Mary sat high atop a camel in the caravan of old Benjamin and his wife as they left Nazareth en route to Jerusalem. Not even the recent disappointing conversations with her parents and Joseph could dampen Mary's enthusiasm. This journey would lead her to the door of her Aunt Elizabeth, and the angel had said her aged aunt was also miraculously expecting a child.

She looked back and waved to her parents before the caravan rounded a curve. "God be with you!" they called.

"And with you!" she responded.

Even at that distance, she could see the worry lines on their faces. And as the caravan made its way across the plain of Esdraelon carrying its bags of grain for the market at Jerusalem, she remembered their discussions of the last week.

"The Messiah will come someday, Mary," her mother had said gently, "but perhaps you've been thinking about it too much."

"Don't you believe me, Mother?" she asked—almost begged.

"I'm just confused, Mary. Just confused," her mother said, shaking her gray head.

"I know you're sincere," her father had said. "But you've always been a dreamer, and this carries things too far."

Even Joseph had not understood. "Mary, I'm eager for the Messiah to come and deliver us from the Romans, too, but we can't dream Him here. Get hold of yourself."

The trip to visit Elizabeth had been her idea, a desperate plea to find someone who would understand, someone who would believe her story.

Her father gladly made arrangements with his old friend Benjamin for her to ride along with him and his wife on their next trip to Jerusalem. As she looked back past the other camels to the fading town of Nazareth, she could almost hear her parents' thoughts, *This trip is the perfect answer. When Mary sees Elizabeth is still barren, she'll realize the whole thing was a dream.*

I guess I can't blame them, Mary thought with a sigh. *They'll understand in time.*

That night they stayed at an inn in Samaria. The following two nights they found similar lodging.

On the fourth morning Mary could hardly contain herself. Today she would see Elizabeth! Today the angel's words would be confirmed. Benjamin made a slight detour from the trade route in order to leave her near Elizabeth's house.

But almost as soon as the caravan turned off the main road, Mary began to have doubts. And as the camels plodded along the back road, she struggled with her thoughts. *What if my parents are right? What if neither I nor Elizabeth is expecting babies after all? What if the angel was a dream?*

No, Mary whispered to herself. *It was not a dream. The angel was real.* In her mind she could still see his dazzling whiteness. She remembered the authority in his voice. *I will believe what he said*, she decided. Then the little home of Elizabeth and Zachariah, nestled among the trees ahead, came into view. Mary's spirits soared again. She could hardly wait to get off the camel. Hurriedly she thanked Benjamin and his wife for their kindness and raced toward the door.

"Elizabeth," she called. "Elizabeth!"

As Elizabeth opened the door, her face bright with excitement, the Holy Spirit came upon her. "Blessed are you among women, and

blessed is the fruit of your womb! . . . As soon as the voice of your greeting sounded in my ears, the babe leaped in my womb for joy. Blessed is she who believed, for there will be a fulfillment of those things which were told her from the Lord."[*]

Oh, it's true, it's true, it's true! Mary whispered. And aloud she joyfully exclaimed:

> My soul magnifies the Lord,
> And my spirit has rejoiced in God my Savior.
> For He has regarded the lowly state of His maidservant;
> For behold, henceforth all generations will call me blessed.
> For He who is mighty has done great things for me.[†]

> *Do you sometimes wonder if God*
> *will do the things He has promised?*
> *If you trust Him, you, like Mary,*
> *will see that God does everything He says He will do.*

The camel is the most difficult figure used in the nativity scene. If you cannot complete it at this point, work through the next several lessons to gain some more experience. The star and the camel share the first few folds, so you may find it helpful to try the camel again after you've mastered the star.

Paper suggestions:
Use origami paper or light weight brown wrapping paper
Size: 9 x 9 inches or larger

---

[*]Luke 1:42–45.
[†]Luke 1:46–49.

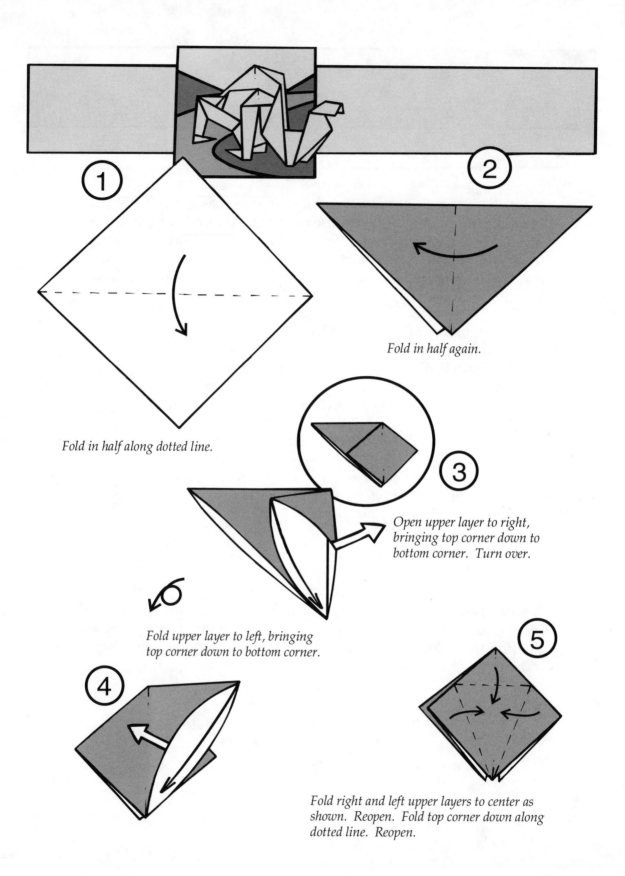

1 Fold in half along dotted line.

2 Fold in half again.

3 Open upper layer to right, bringing top corner down to bottom corner. Turn over.

Fold upper layer to left, bringing top corner down to bottom corner.

4

5 Fold right and left upper layers to center as shown. Reopen. Fold top corner down along dotted line. Reopen.

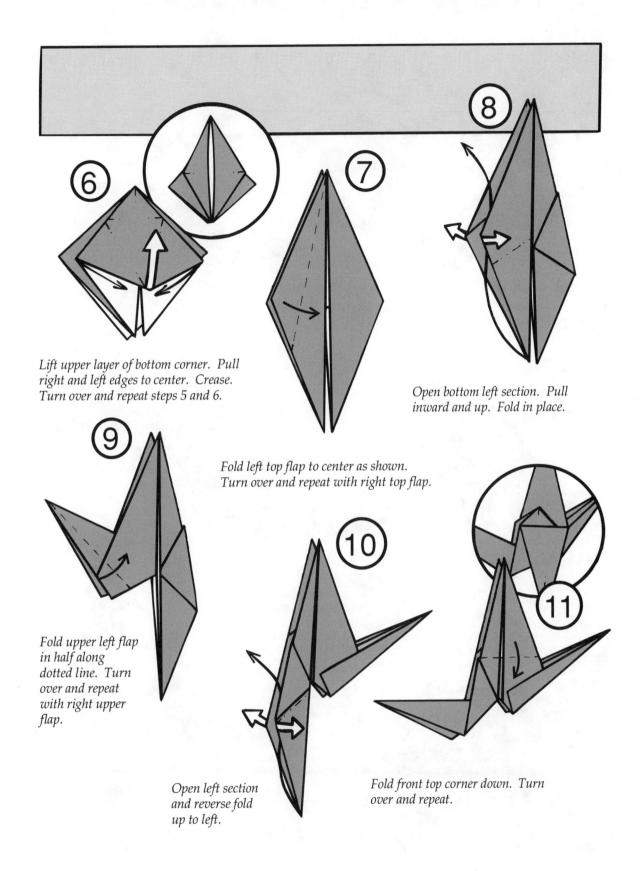

6 Lift upper layer of bottom corner. Pull right and left edges to center. Crease. Turn over and repeat steps 5 and 6.

7 Fold left top flap to center as shown. Turn over and repeat with right top flap.

8 Open bottom left section. Pull inward and up. Fold in place.

9 Fold upper left flap in half along dotted line. Turn over and repeat with right upper flap.

10 Open left section and reverse fold up to left.

11 Fold front top corner down. Turn over and repeat.

23 ———

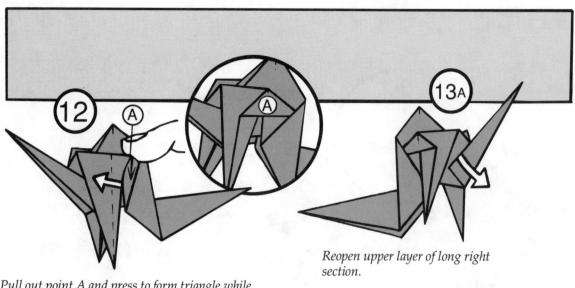

Pull out point A and press to form triangle while folding front flap along dotted line. Turn over. Repeat.

Reopen upper layer of long right section.

Fold upper layer (flap B) down along dotted line.

Lift leg and flap B will unfold. Tuck it underneath leg. Turn over and repeat steps 13 and 14.

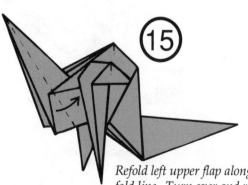

Refold left upper flap along previous fold line. Turn over and repeat with right upper flap.

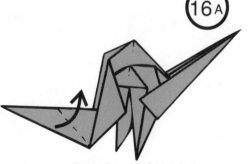

To make neck fold left section up along dotted line. Unfold.

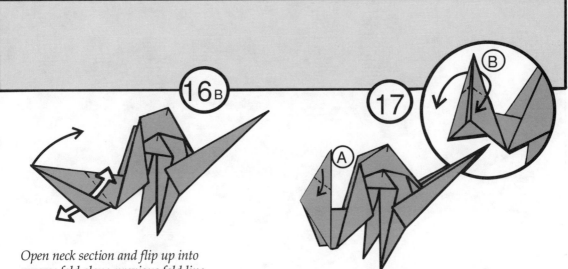

Open neck section and flip up into
reverse fold along previous fold line.

A. Fold neck section down along dotted line.
Reopen. B. Reverse fold along fold line to form
head.

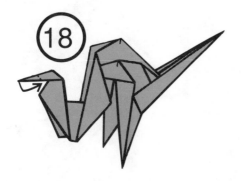

Fold point on head inside.

Fold right section down along dotted
line. Reopen. Place thumb inside right
section and reverse fold down.

Fold legs under so camel will kneel.

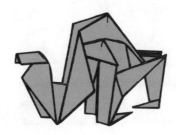

Joseph's Visitor

All day long Joseph agonized over his problem as he worked in his carpenter shop, sanding a chair for the rabbi. Mary, his betrothed, was pregnant. Oh, she had told him of the angel's promise before she left for Judea. Like her parents, though, he assumed she had only imagined the angel's visit.

Now after three months, she was back, claiming that her original story was correct. But how? By whom? *Not by him!* They had hardly even *talked* alone.

How could he marry an unfaithful girl? But was sweet, sensitive Mary *that* kind of girl? He hadn't thought so. What if she was right about the angel's visit? But such a thing had never happened before. She was just overwrought. But she was pregnant. How? By whom?

His thoughts raced on and on in a circle without resolution. He ate no supper, despite his long day of work. The sun set. Darkness fell. The moon came out. Still Joseph paced.

What was to be done? The punishment for unfaithfulness was death by stoning. He'd seen a stoning once. The man had robbed a caravan and killed some of the people. Even so, the stoning had been a gruesome thing to watch. Mary stoned? He couldn't bear the thought! But what was to be done? He couldn't marry an unfaithful girl. Perhaps he could just quietly have the engagement annulled.

If only I had the wisdom of God, he thought as he prepared for bed. Wasn't there a proverb that promised God's direction to those who trusted Him? Yes, he remembered it from synagogue school.

Trust in the LORD with all your heart,
And lean not on your own understanding;
In all your ways acknowledge Him,
And He shall direct your paths.[*]

"I need Your wisdom," he whispered as he crawled onto his sleeping mat. "I really need Your wisdom." Then he drifted into a restless sleep.

"Joseph!" It was an angel.

"Do not be afraid to take to you Mary your wife, for that which is conceived in her is of the Holy Spirit. And she will bring forth a Son, and you shall call His name JESUS, for He will save His people from their sins."[†]

Joseph jumped up, instantly awake! *The angel—where is he? Gone! I have so many more questions I want to ask him!* But the angel had said all that was really necessary. Mary had told the truth. His anxiety melted away.

Mary was indeed the special girl he had thought—more special than he'd ever dreamed! God had chosen her too—as mother of the Messiah. *And me? I'm chosen as well,* he realized, *to watch after the Christ Child and help Him grow up.*

Then he remembered his prayer for wisdom. God had answered it. Somehow, he knew he'd pray that prayer many times as he helped rear the Messiah.

Joseph was at Mary's house before breakfast the next morning to tell her and her parents the good news. He had seen an angel too! He'd gladly take Mary as his wife and assume responsibility for rearing her child.

*When you have a problem, you too can
ask God to show you what to do,
just as Joseph did.*

---

[*]Proverbs 3:5–6.
[†]Matthew 1:20b, 21.

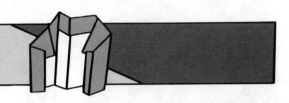

✳

The wise men will look like Joseph. Since this is a very easy figure, you may want to make the wise men at this time.

Paper suggestions:
Joseph: Origami or wrapping paper
Size: 8 x 8 inches

Wise men: Brightly colored wrapping or origami paper
Size: 9 x 9 inches

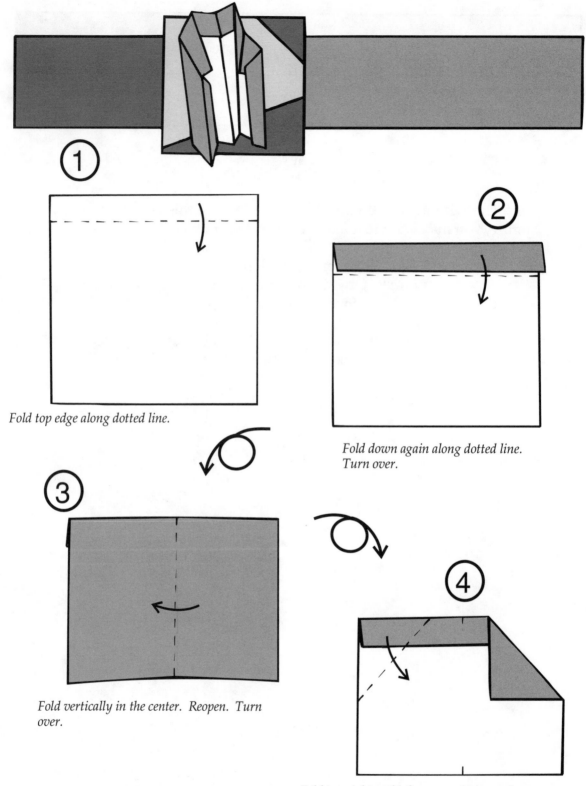

① Fold top edge along dotted line.

② Fold down again along dotted line. Turn over.

③ Fold vertically in the center. Reopen. Turn over.

④ Fold top right and left corners down as shown.

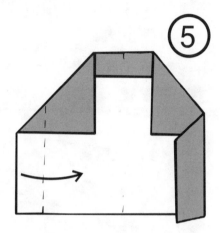

Fold right and left edges along dotted lines.

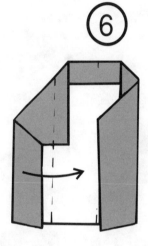

Fold right and left sides to center.

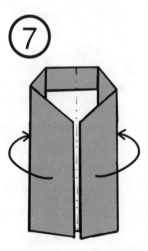

Fold right and left sides backward along center line and stand up.

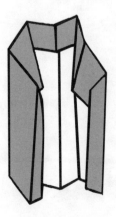

An Unexpected Journey

J oseph was bargaining for some nails in the marketplace when it happened. A Roman captain raced into the center of town, dismounted his horse, unrolled a scroll and read. "Every Jewish man is ordered to report to the city of his birth to register for taxes." The captain rolled up his scroll, mounted his horse and was off to the next town leaving a cloud of doom upon his hearers.

"Taxes!" Joseph exploded. "We're *already* taxed beyond endurance!"

Townspeople around him shouted angrily after the captain. A rabbi, standing nearby, looked at Joseph, and said, "Someday, the Messiah will come and deliver us from the Romans."

The Messiah, yes, thought Joseph, remembering the baby growing within Mary's womb. *And just how am I to leave her at this important time for a trip to Bethlehem, the city of my birth?* Mary's baby was due within a month. He picked up his box of nails and hurried home.

That night, as they ate the evening meal, he told Mary the sad news. She didn't cry or feel sorry for herself, as some young girls would have. Her decision was quick and firm. "I'll go with you," she said.

"Mary, it's seventy miles. Seventy miles on a donkey and you expecting the baby at anytime. What if the Messiah is born on the road somewhere?"

"God will take care of the Messiah," she said simply.

Joseph stared at her but did not argue with her. But, to himself, he said, *I thought God gave me that job.*

And that's how it happened that two weeks later he strapped a flask of water, a bag of dried fruit, a loaf of hard bread and some cheese to Molith, their donkey. Mary had packed a few strips of cloth for the infant who was sure to be born before their return.

She alternately rode the donkey and walked along with Joseph. *Oh, Lord,* Joseph whispered, *don't let any harm come to her. Women sometimes die in childbirth. And the Messiah, what about Him? What if something bad were to happen to Him?*

And where will we stay when we reach Bethlehem? he wondered. *Has a man ever encountered so many problems when he got married? If only we didn't have to make this trip, at least not now.*

They were not alone on the journey; others joined them along the road, some going to Jerusalem, Jericho, Emmaus, or Bethany. Decrees from Caesar Augustus had to be obeyed. That night they were able to find lodging in an obscure town of Samaria. Before Joseph snuffed out the lamp, Mary whispered, "Remember the prophecy about the Messiah?"

"You mean the one about His being born of a virgin?"

"No, the one about *where* He will be born," she said with the earnestness that was so characteristic of her.

The words from the prophet Micah flooded Joseph's memory: "'But you, Bethlehem . . . out of you shall come forth . . . the One to be Ruler in Israel.'* *Bethlehem . . . Bethlehem!*" he exclaimed.

Even Caesar Augustus could not stop God's plan for the Messiah. In fact, God was using this exasperating tax business to get them to Bethlehem.

"Thank You, God for being in control. I know You will take care of Mary and the Messiah too," Joseph whispered before he fell asleep.

---

*Micah 5:2a.

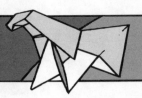

Do you sometimes wonder why things happen as they do?
It's not always easy to trust God when trouble comes,
but He uses even bad things to bring about good in the end.

Paper suggestions:
Origami paper or thin brown wrapping paper
Size: 6 x 6 inches

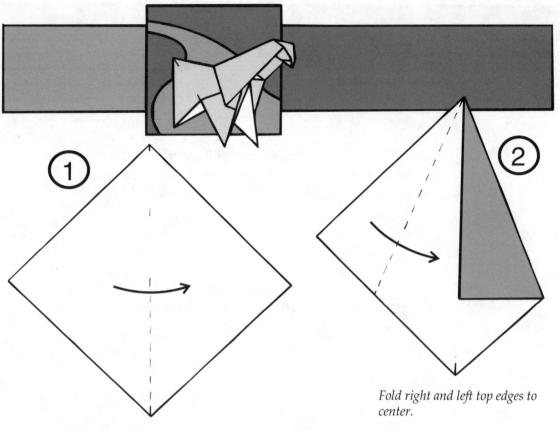

① Fold left corner to right along center and reopen.

② Fold right and left top edges to center.

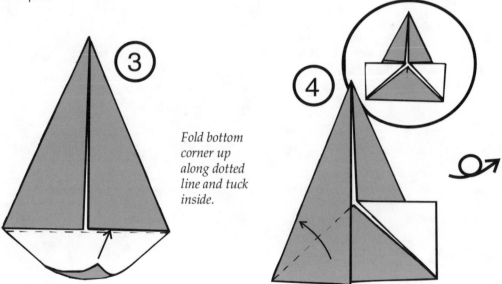

③ Fold bottom corner up along dotted line and tuck inside.

④ Fold right and left flaps to outside. Turn over.

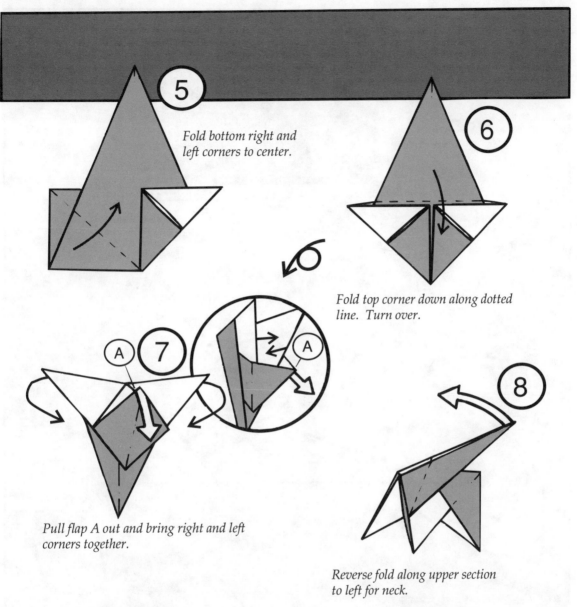

5 Fold bottom right and left corners to center.

6 Fold top corner down along dotted line. Turn over.

7 Pull flap A out and bring right and left corners together.

8 Reverse fold along upper section to left for neck.

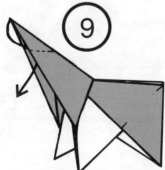

9 Fold end section inside and down to form head.

10 Fold tip inside.

The Shining Moment

Late the next afternoon, Joseph looked at the horizon and sighed. The barren hills of Samaria stretched ahead as far as he could see. *Will we ever reach Bethlehem?* he wondered.

Mary was tired. Her steps were slow. When she rode the donkey, she kept adjusting her position and rubbing her back. She didn't complain, though, and she would hardly stop, even for food or a drink of water.

The third day of their journey, however, she awoke refreshed, her energy renewed. Joseph was amazed at how quickly she moved, how eagerly she started the day's journey. Of course, they anticipated they would reach Bethlehem that night. Perhaps that accounted for her eagerness.

They made good time until the sun was almost overhead, when Mary suddenly became tired. "Maybe a little food will strengthen you," Joseph suggested.

She nodded. But the dried fish and figs did not refresh her. And when they started on again, their progress was slower than ever. Once Joseph noticed Mary holding her robe around her abdomen as if she were in pain.

"How are you doing?" he asked, laying a reassuring hand on her shoulder.

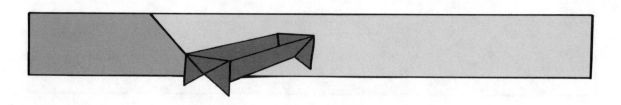

She managed a smile, but her face was pale. He worried even more. Bethlehem was still miles away. Would they make it in time? He had hoped they could arrive by sunset, find a room, and get settled before nightfall. They followed the trade route through Jerusalem, resisting the temptation to stay in one of the many inns there. They must reach Bethlehem before the Child's birth.

Mary rubbed her back more often as they left the city and began the descent toward the little town. By the time they reached the well at the edge of town, the evening star had risen in the night sky. Joseph stopped for only a moment to draw a quick drink of fresh water for each of them.

He was too concerned about the crowds moving along the main street to linger. *Where are all these people spending the night?* he wondered as he made his way to the only inn.

"Sorry, I'm filled up," said the gray-haired owner in answer to his question. "Not a space left."

Then he saw the worry on the traveler's face and looked past Joseph to the young woman on the donkey. Her time was obviously near. She could hardly have her baby on the street, so he led them to the cave behind the house that served as a stable.

"It's clean," he said. "The stable boy takes care of that. It shelters the sheep and the cows when they have their young. Never had a baby here before, but then, the town's never been this crowded either. The hay's in the corner. Use what you need to make yourselves comfortable." Then, before he disappeared out the door, he added, "I'll tell my wife you'll be needing some help after a while."

Glad for even this protection from the night's chill, Joseph hurriedly gathered some hay into a heap. Then he spread his cloak for Mary to stretch out on. Perspiration beaded her forehead as she eased herself onto the makeshift bed. The innkeeper's red-faced wife arrived shortly, offering to help the baby into the world.

Sometime around midnight a donkey stirred in his stall. A lamb bleated and snuggled up to his mother. And a baby cried. A moment later the innkeeper's wife laid a son in Mary's arms.

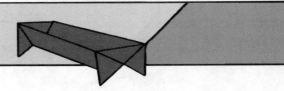

Joseph bent over him and gazed in wonder at the Child. "We'll call Him Jesus," he said, his voice husky, "just like the angel commanded."

Mary nodded, her eyes glistening with joy. "The Son of God," she whispered. But she said no more and Joseph knew her heart was too full for words.

It seemed impossible, but the ancient prophecy had come true. A virgin had given birth to a Son. Then, as Joseph watched, Mary lovingly cradled the Christ Child against her and bent to kiss His forehead.

The birth of a baby is the most miraculous event in human experience.
Each child is a special gift from our Creator.
Baby Jesus, however, was special in a different way:
He was the Son of God.

Paper Suggestions:
Origami paper, brown wrapping paper, or other
rugged-looking paper
Size: 4 x 5 1/2 inches

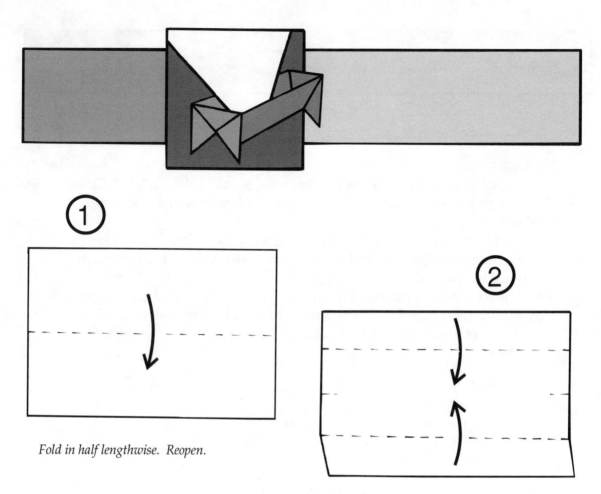

① Fold in half lengthwise. Reopen.

② Fold bottom edge to center. Repeat with top edge.

③ Fold all corners as shown. Reopen.

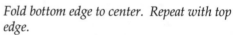

④

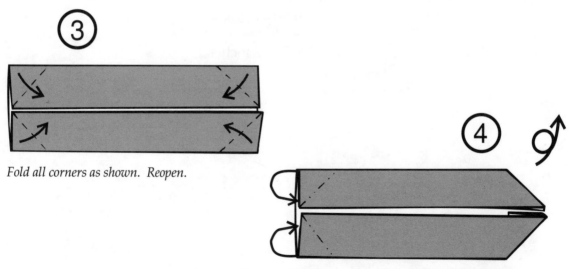

Reverse fold all four corners to inside. Turn over.

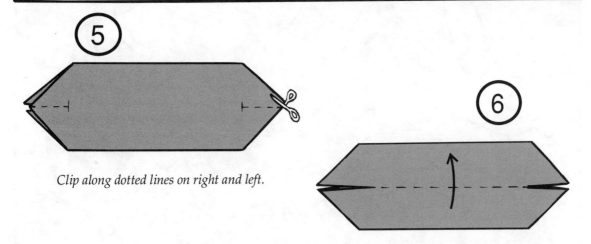

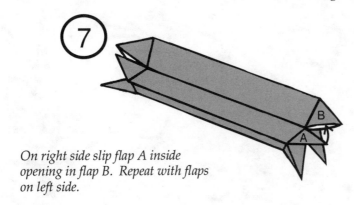

④ 5

Clip along dotted lines on right and left.

⑥ 6

Fold lengthwise bottom to top. Reopen.

⑦ 7

On right side slip flap A inside
opening in flap B. Repeat with flaps
on left side.

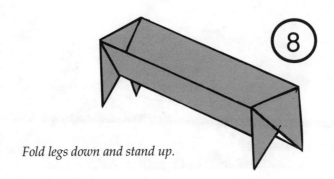

⑧ 8

Fold legs down and stand up.

The Shepherds' Surprise

Josh shivered and snuggled deep into his ragged sheepskin cover as he edged closer to the fire. He'd often wondered why the shepherds didn't bring the sheep in at night, but Grandfather only laughed at him. "It's rarely cold in Bethlehem," he said. "It hasn't snowed in five years, and then it hardly covered the ground and was gone the next day."

"The town's sure crowded tonight," he heard Grandfather say now.

"It's that blasted tax," replied his Uncle Reu. "When I signed up yesterday, I thought the collection agent was going to demand half my flock. What right do they have to tax us so heavily that we can hardly feed our children, anyway? What do we get out of it?"

"Easy, Reu. Someday they won't. Someday the Messiah—"

"Someday, *someday!*" retorted Reu. "That's all I ever hear. *Someday* the Messiah will come! When? It's *now* we need Him!"

"The rabbis say the time is right. It could be soon," Grandfather replied patiently.

As Josh dozed off, he heard his father say, "It's here in Bethlehem He will be born."

Josh's eyes popped open. His father and the other shepherds had fallen to the ground and were crying out in terror. In midair above them stood the whitest creature Josh had ever seen. A bright light streamed from him illuminating the whole hillside.

"Do not be afraid," he called out, "for behold, I bring you good tidings of great joy which will be to all people. For there is born to you this day in the city of David a Savior, who is Christ the Lord."[*] The angel paused as if to give them time to take in what he had said. Then he continued, "You will find a Babe wrapped in swaddling cloths, lying in a manger."[†]

Suddenly the sky pulsed with thousands of beings similar to the first, joyously singing praises to God. Josh watched them, his mouth open. He often lingered to hear the temple choirs when he delivered lambs for the sacrifices. But the beauty and harmony of this heavenly chorus far exceeded anything he had ever heard.

"Glory to God in the highest," they sang, "and on earth peace, goodwill toward men!"[‡] Over and over these words rang out in a joyous pronouncement of some blessing Josh did not fully understand. The last strains of their song drifted to him as the angels trailed into the night toward the stars.

Uncle Reu was the first to recover his composure after the heavenly beings were gone. "Come on," he said. "Let's go find Him!"

"Go see the Savior—the Messiah—dressed in rags and smelling like a sheep pen?" asked Josh's father. "And who will stay with the sheep?"

"The sheep?" Uncle Reu asked. Plainly he had forgotten all about them.

"The sheep will be fine," Grandfather said. "The angel told us to go."

---

[*]Luke 2:10b, 11.
[†]Luke 2:12b.
[‡]Luke 2:14.

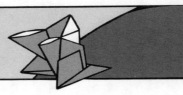

"He must be in the stable behind the inn," Uncle Reu said excitedly, as they hurried along the path to town. "But why a stable? The Messiah should have a palace."

"And why were poor shepherds like us told about such an important event?" Josh's father wondered aloud.

All those questions whirled about in Josh's mind, too, as he ran ahead. When he rounded the bend toward the stable, the innkeeper's wife was just leaving. She had an excitement about her he'd never seen before. "Is He in there?" Josh asked.

She nodded.

When Josh pushed open the stable door, he saw a young couple bending over a manger. Their faces glowed with joy.

Josh suddenly felt embarrassed, as if he'd burst in upon a very private event. But when he started to edge out the door, it creaked.

The man looked up. "Did you want something?" he asked kindly.

Josh hesitated, but Uncle Reu, who had squeezed inside behind him, spoke right up. "Yes, we came to see the Messiah." His eyes shone, and his voice rose as he continued: "The angels told us about Him."

"Angels?" the man asked, but he didn't seem at all surprised.

"They said He'd be in a manger."

"And they sang a wonderful song," put in Josh. "Oh, please, may we see Him?"

The woman looked up then and motioned them forward.

Josh edged close to the manger and peeked inside. There, all snuggled in a white cloth, lay a tiny baby, the newest one he'd ever seen. "Is it Him? Is He the Messiah?" he asked.

The woman smiled and nodded. "His name is Jesus, the Savior," she said. "It's the name the angel gave Him."

"The Messiah!" Josh whispered in awe and knelt before Him.

"He has come after all," he heard Uncle Reu say as he knelt down too.

"Praise God!" Father and Grandfather exclaimed as they also dropped to their knees.

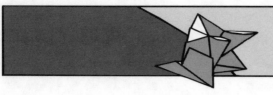

When the shepherds finally tore themselves away from the stable, light was dawning in the eastern sky and Bethlehem was already astir. Josh ran home to tell his mother and sisters what had happened. Uncle Reu and Josh's father were soon talking about it to the shopkeepers.

A stream of visitors carrying small offerings of everything from goat cheese to outgrown baby clothes was soon on its way to the stable.

By the time Josh and the other shepherds returned to the sheep, it was midmorning, but not a single lamb was missing.

You'd think that a king would be born in a palace, but not Jesus, the Messiah. He came to a poor family, and He still cares about ordinary people like you and me.

Paper Suggestions:
Origami paper or wrapping paper
Size: 10 x 10 inches or larger for men,
7 x 7 inches for child

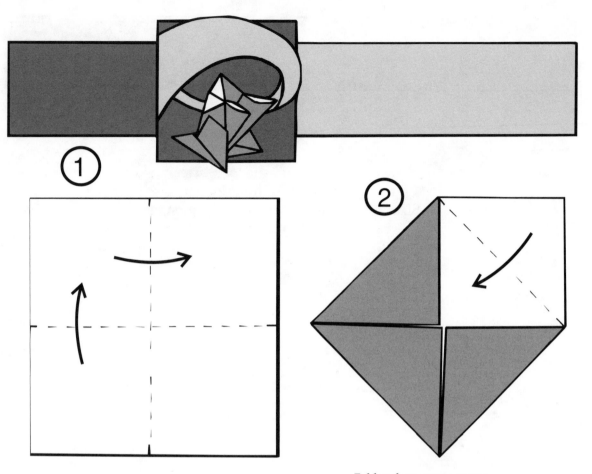

1

Fold in half vertically. Reopen. Fold in half horizontally. Reopen.

2

Fold each corner to center.

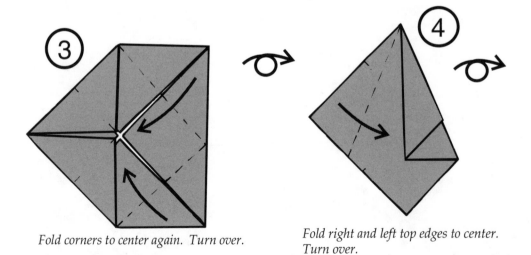

3

Fold corners to center again. Turn over.

4

Fold right and left top edges to center. Turn over.

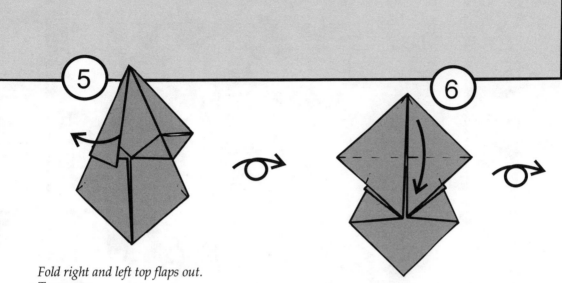

Fold right and left top flaps out.
Turn over.

Fold top corner down along dotted line, being sure
flap on back flips up for head. Turn over.

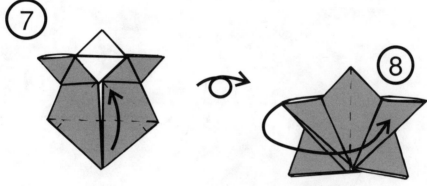

Fold bottom corner up. Turn over.

Fold left side to right along center dotted
line.

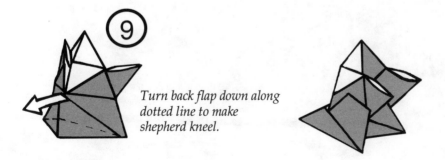

Turn back flap down along
dotted line to make
shepherd kneel.

A Visit to the Temple

Forty days after the birth of the first son in a Jewish family it was customary for the parents to present him to God at the temple and for the mother to go through a purification ceremony there.

Mary sang a lullaby as she wrapped Baby Jesus in fresh swaddling cloths for their journey to Jerusalem. "It's Your dedication day, Your first visit to Your Father's house, and You mustn't cry," she whispered. Then she lifted Jesus to her shoulder and went to meet Joseph, who had brought Molith around to the door. Joseph helped her mount the little donkey and led them down Bethlehem's main street and onto the road to Jerusalem.

Once they were out in the country, Joseph's brow wrinkled. "I wish I had a better offering for you to present than these two little turtledoves," he said sadly. "The mother of the Messiah deserves a lamb."

"God must care more about people's attitudes than the size of their gifts," Mary replied. "Otherwise, He wouldn't have chosen us in the first place."

"It's certain that God doesn't do things the way we'd expect," Joseph agreed.

Mary looked at Jesus, lulled to sleep by the rhythmic motion of the donkey. Then her eyes strayed across the hills toward Nazareth.

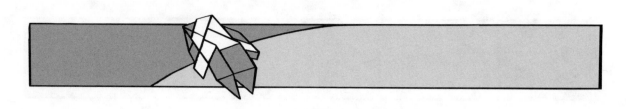

She thought of her mother and father, of Ruth and the daily trips to the well. Loneliness crept uninvited into her heart. "I wish my parents could be here to see Jesus dedicated," she said. "As it is, we'll be all by ourselves."

But once they entered Jerusalem, Mary forgot her loneliness. And when they reached the temple area, activity filled the air. Herod's workmen were everywhere measuring, digging footings for columns, and laying tile. "He's trying to buy our loyalty by building us a magnificent temple," Joseph commented. "I wonder what God thinks of his efforts."

Joseph found a place to tether Molith and helped Mary dismount. As they made their way across the temple courts, a very old man named Simeon approached them. "May I hold the child?" he asked earnestly.

Mary looked at him carefully, hesitating. But the man was so intent, his face beaming with excitement, that she laid Jesus gently into his arms. Simeon looked lovingly at the child and then raised his face to heaven,

> "Lord, now You are letting Your servant depart in peace,
> According to Your word;
> For my eyes have seen Your salvation."[*]

Then he looked at the astonished parents and blessed them. Turning to Mary, he said, "This Child is destined for the fall and rising of many in Israel, and for a sign which will be spoken against (yes, a sword will pierce through your own soul also), that the thoughts of many hearts may be revealed."[†]

While he spoke, an old lady hurried up to them. "Praise be to the Lord," she said. "Praise be to the Lord! He has sent the Messiah at last! God has answered our prayers!"

---

[*]Luke 2:29, 30.
[†]Luke 2:34, 35a.

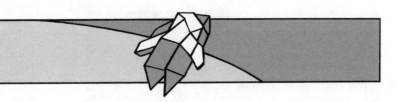

She continued praising the Lord as she accompanied them to the dedication. "This is the Messiah for whom I have fasted and prayed many years," she told everyone they met.

Returning to Bethlehem at sunset, both Mary and Joseph were quiet. Mary looked again toward Nazareth, "This morning I was worried about being alone in the temple, and God sent those dear old people to be with us," she finally commented.

"How did they know?" asked Joseph, puzzled. "How did they know Jesus is the Messiah?"

Mary shook her head. "I don't know—a vision, maybe? A word from God?" After a while she said, "Simeon's message troubles me. I really don't understand. Why will being the mother of the Messiah bring a sword to my heart?"

Joseph thought a few minutes as they traveled along by an olive grove. "Rome won't give up easily," he replied finally. "There's sure to be bloodshed if the Messiah sets up an earthly kingdom. Maybe that's what he meant." Then seeing Mary's worried eyes he continued. "It won't be easy. It hasn't been so far."

Mary nodded thoughtfully. "But the Messiah has come. That's what matters, isn't it?"

Joseph nodded. "We'll have to keep trusting God for the future."

Mary cuddled Baby Jesus a little closer as they approached Bethlehem.

Mary and Joseph knew that God would care for them and that
He would be with them when painful times came.
He'll do the same for us.

Paper Suggestions:
White or light colored origami or typing paper
Size: 4 x 4 inches

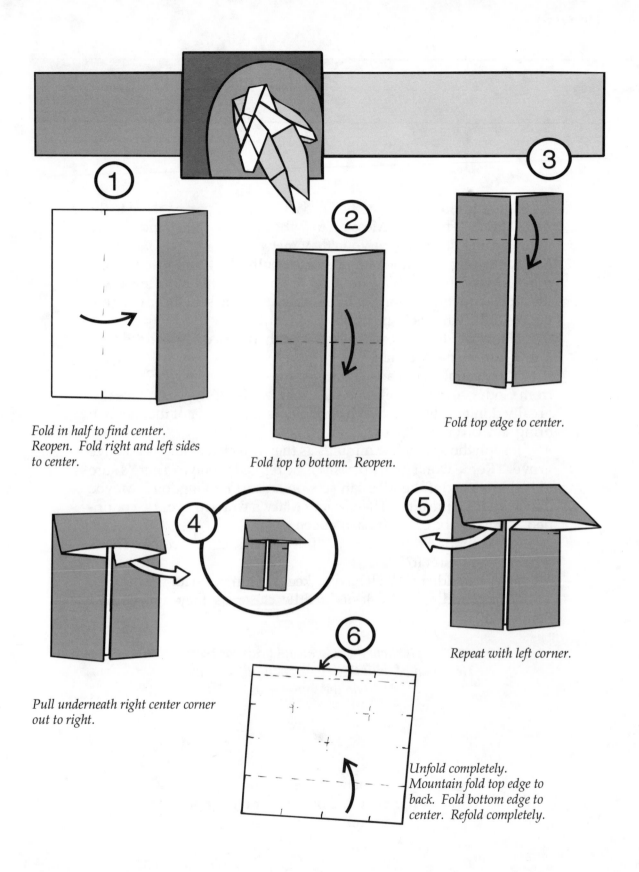

1. Fold in half to find center. Reopen. Fold right and left sides to center.

2. Fold top to bottom. Reopen.

3. Fold top edge to center.

4. Pull underneath right center corner out to right.

5. Repeat with left corner.

6. Unfold completely. Mountain fold top edge to back. Fold bottom edge to center. Refold completely.

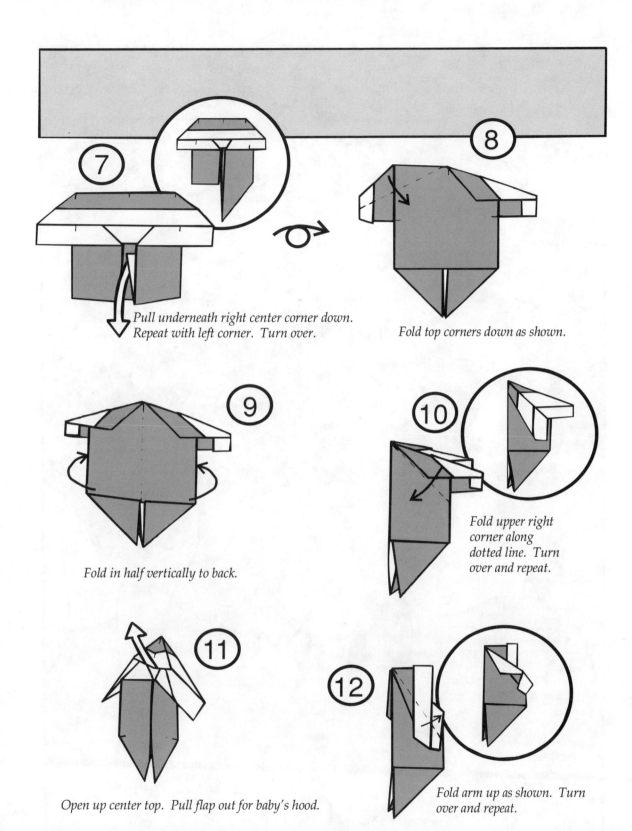

⑦ Pull underneath right center corner down. Repeat with left corner. Turn over.

⑧ Fold top corners down as shown.

⑨ Fold in half vertically to back.

⑩ Fold upper right corner along dotted line. Turn over and repeat.

⑪ Open up center top. Pull flap out for baby's hood.

⑫ Fold arm up as shown. Turn over and repeat.

Wise Men and a Star

Far away in eastern lands lived a group of wise men who studied ancient scrolls. The Jewish people, they read, had been promised a very special king called the Messiah. He would be the Son of God, and would bring all people inner peace and joy. They had no peace in their religion. How they hoped this king would be born during their lifetime!

Then one winter night as they were rolling up their manuscripts to go to bed, a star blazed forth over Palestine. It was the largest, brightest star they had ever seen.

"This must be the sign that the Jewish king has been born," they decided. And, more than anything else, they wanted to see Him.

They remembered how far it was to Palestine. They remembered the hot desert they would have to cross and the robbers hiding in the ravines. But in their desire to see this wonderful king, they decided to go anyway.

Preparations began the very next day. Their servants gathered dried foods and nuts for the long trip. They prepared the wise men's clothes and checked to make sure the camels were in good shape.

What kind of gift is valuable enough for a baby King? they wondered.

"Gold," said one wise man.

"Frankincense," said another.

"Myrrh," said a third.

They put their gifts in elegant containers, the most beautiful ones available. Then they arose early one morning and set off in a caravan across the desert.

Weeks passed. They grew tired. Their bones ached from the constant motion of the camels, and the hot sand cut into their skin. Their clean clothes were no longer clean, and everything smelled of camel. But they didn't complain, for with every step the camels took, they were closer to Palestine and the baby King.

After months of travel, the wise men arrived in Jerusalem. They headed straight for the palace. It never occurred to them that the infant King would be anywhere else. Strangely King Herod didn't look happy about their news. But when he had talked with his own counselors, he discovered that the Messiah was to be born in Bethlehem.

Once again on the road, the wise men wondered how they would find the right house and the right child. They had come so far. Was it possible that they would not know which baby in Bethlehem was the Messiah?

As they neared Bethlehem, evening shadows crept over the countryside, and the stars came out. Then to their great joy, they saw the star they had seen in their own land. It hung over Bethlehem like a giant lantern. They followed its light down the ancient streets until it stopped above one very small house. They knew their journey had ended.

Have you ever started a project that became
more difficult as you went along, until it seemed impossible?
If so, you know a little about how the wise men felt.
But if you don't give up, you too will reach your goal.

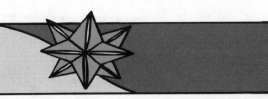

Paper Suggestions:
Gold or silver origami paper or Christmas wrap
Size: 6 x 6 inches

If you have not already completed the wise men, you may want to
complete them now.

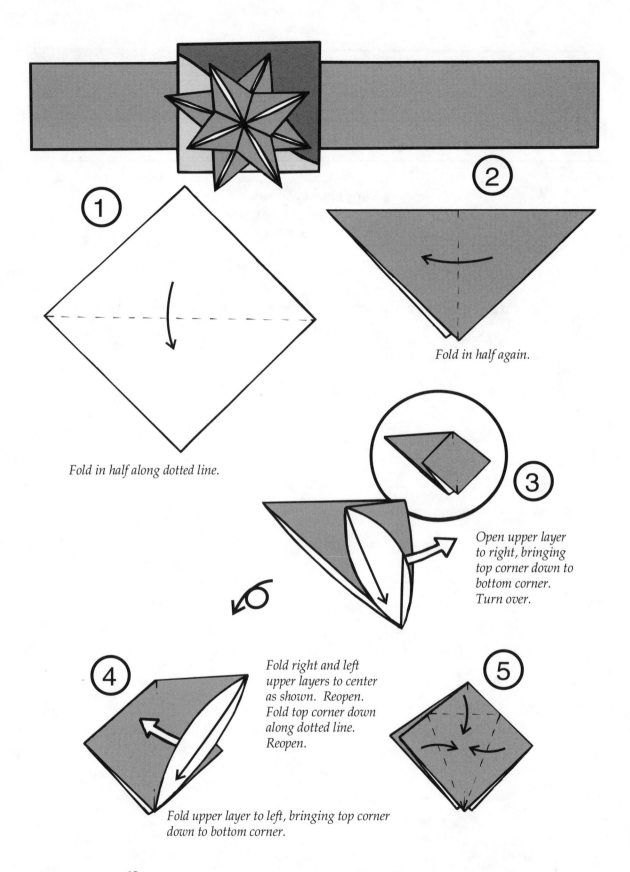

① Fold in half along dotted line.

② Fold in half again.

③ Open upper layer to right, bringing top corner down to bottom corner. Turn over.

④ Fold right and left upper layers to center as shown. Reopen. Fold top corner down along dotted line. Reopen.

Fold upper layer to left, bringing top corner down to bottom corner.

⑤

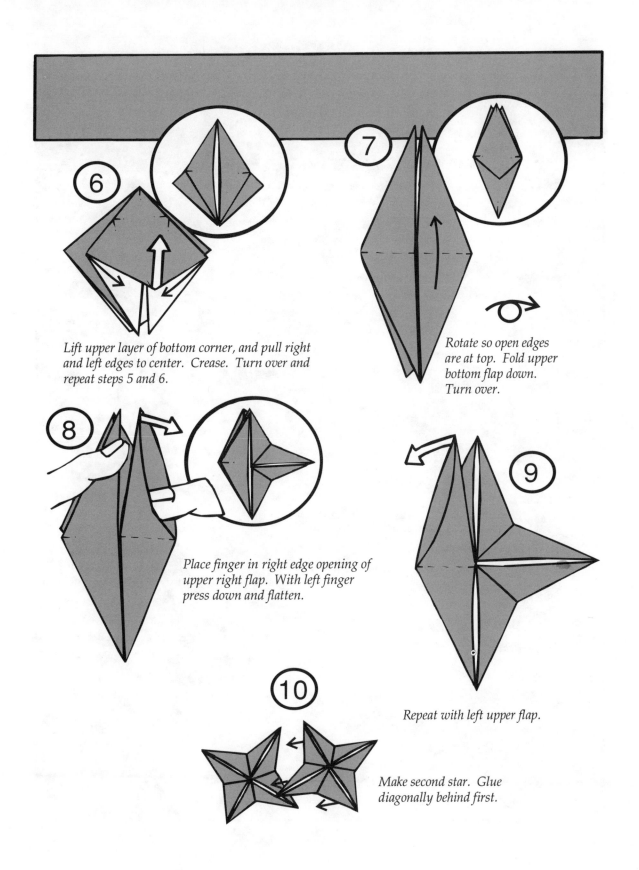

6 Lift upper layer of bottom corner, and pull right and left edges to center. Crease. Turn over and repeat steps 5 and 6.

7 Rotate so open edges are at top. Fold upper bottom flap down. Turn over.

8 Place finger in right edge opening of upper right flap. With left finger press down and flatten.

9 Repeat with left upper flap.

10 Make second star. Glue diagonally behind first.

God Protects
the Infant King

The Holy Family settled in Bethlehem. Joseph found work as a carpenter once again, and Mary tended Jesus and the needs of the household.

One evening, when Jesus was almost two years old, Joseph looked out the door to find a whole caravan arriving at his home. Had they mistaken his tiny house for the inn?

When he started to direct them to the inn down the street, however, the elegantly dressed spokesman bowed and pointed to the star above the house. "Is this the home of the Jewish King about whom we have read in ancient writings?"

Taken aback, Joseph nodded.

"We have traveled far to worship Him," the traveler explained.

So Joseph opened the door wide as the wise men trooped in, their robes trailing behind them.

Mary, a little aghast at their splendor, picked up Jesus from where He had been playing on the floor. The wise men knelt before Him, wonder upon their faces, and worshiped the King for whom they had endured sand and wind and desert heat. Then they unloaded their precious gifts before the astonished eyes of Mary and Joseph.

Two nights after the mysterious visit from the wise men, Joseph awoke in a cold sweat. "Mary, Mary," he cried shaking his sleepy wife. "Get up! We must leave immediately! An angel just came to me in a dream. He said King Herod will try to kill the Child. We must leave the country! The angel said we must travel to Egypt." As he lit the lamp and began gathering their few belongings together, Joseph made plans aloud. "We'll go to Gaza and take a ship to Alexandria."

Mary sat up and began to take in what was happening. "Joseph, it takes money to live in Egypt. It's not like Israel, and we've nothing even for passage," she reminded him. Then she remembered the wise men's gifts. A glimmer of understanding went through her. "The provision of Jehovah to meet our needs in a foreign land," she whispered gratefully.

She stood up and slipped on her robe. Then she lovingly picked up Jesus and wrapped a warm cloak about Him.

Joseph was already packing Molith for the journey. He helped Mary onto the faithful beast and handed the Baby to her. Then he led them through the dark streets toward the road to Gaza.

"God will take care of us," Mary told the Child, as she settled Him against her. And she knew He would.

Families often face moves and changes today that are frightening too.
But if we ask God to stay with us, He will,
just as He was with the Holy Family.

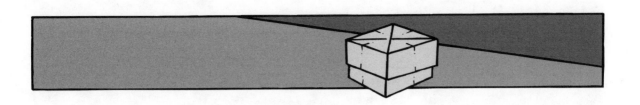

Paper Suggestions:
Foil Christmas wrap (red, gold, silver) or origami paper
Size: 2 gifts 3 x 3 inches,
1 gift 4 x 4 inches

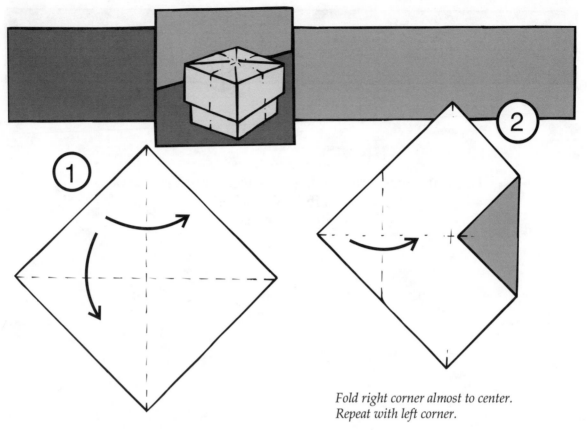

1 Fold top corner to bottom. Reopen. Fold left corner to right. Reopen.

2 Fold right corner almost to center. Repeat with left corner.

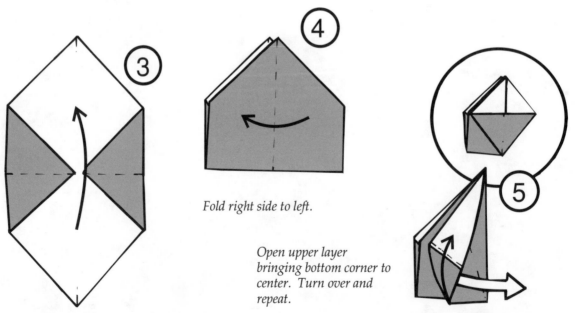

3 Fold bottom corner to top corner.

4 Fold right side to left.

5 Open upper layer bringing bottom corner to center. Turn over and repeat.

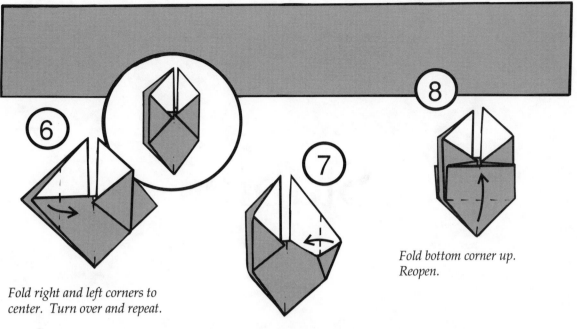

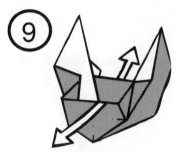

Fold right and left corners to center. Turn over and repeat.

Reopen right and left corners and fold inside toward center. Turn over. Repeat.

Fold bottom corner up. Reopen.

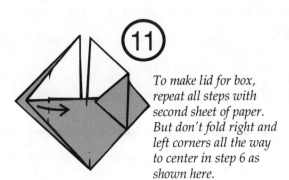

Grasp front and back sides. Pull apart carefully to form box.

Fold top corners inside box.

To make lid for box, repeat all steps with second sheet of paper. But don't fold right and left corners all the way to center in step 6 as shown here.

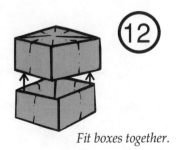

Fit boxes together.

Stable

Materials: Utility knife
              Ruler
              Masking tape or hot glue
              24" x 16" Corrugated cardboard

1. *On back side of cardboard, measure and mark 4 inches from right and left bottom edges.*

2. *At 4-inch marks measure straight up 8 inches and draw line.*

3. *On right and left edges measure up 9 1/2 inches and mark.*

4. *On right and left edges measure up 10 1/2 inches and mark.*

5. *From 10 1/2 inches mark, draw line to center top on right side. Repeat on left. Cut along these lines.*

6. *Draw a line from point D to point E that is parallel to line A-B. Do likewise from point E to F.*

7. *Measure and mark 1 1/4 inches from points A and C toward center top. Cut out shaded wedges.*

8. *Measure and mark 3/4 inch down from center top on each side. Cut out shaded wedge.*

9. *Cut part way through cardboard from points G to D to E to F to H.*

10. *Turn over and fold flaps forward to form stable. Tape or glue flaps in place.*

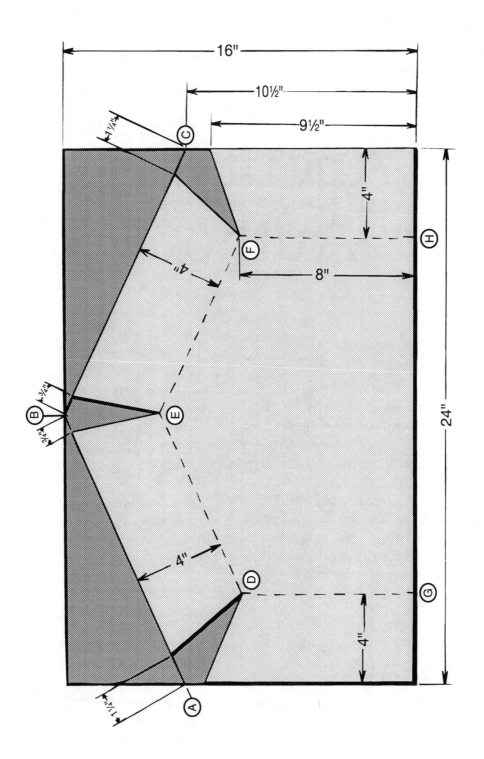

About the Author

Geneva Iijima and her husband, Peter, were part of the U. S. Embassy in Tokyo in the 1970s. While there Geneva fell in love with the origami crafts their children brought home from school, and she began learning the folds too. Geneva brought the gift of origami back to the U. S., and she and her children began teaching it in community classes for fun.

Today Geneva's four children are grown, but she continues to teach, and she weaves origami and her experiences in Japan into her freelance writing. She is active in her hometown of Oregon City, Oregon, and coordinates area Moms in Touch groups.